The Love Songs of Ephram Pratt

Poems

The Love Songs
of Ephram Pratt

Poems

Jack e Lorts

First U.S. edition 2019

Editor and Publisher: Laura LeHew

Proofreaders: Nancy Carol Moody
                        Roy R. Seitz

Cover Art: "E-#12" © Robert Tomlinson

Robert Tomlinson has served as executive director and curator for The San Jose Institute for Contemporary Art, Gallery One Visual Arts Center and the Oregon Arts Alliance. He has curated and installed over 100 exhibitions and created a gallery for the developmentally disabled. A working artist, Tomlinson has conducted his own studio practice for over 40 years. In 2011 he co-founded 13 Hats, a group of artist and writers that collaborated for two years on a wide range of creative projects and exhibitions. His work has been featured in 35 solo shows and over 50 group exhibitions.

Uttered Chaos
PO Box 50638
Eugene, OR 97405
www.utteredchaos.org

ISBN: 978-0-9998334-5-2

for Celia

"The fact that I myself do not understand what my paintings mean while I am painting them does not imply that they are meaningless."

~Salvador Dali

CONTENTS

EPHRAM PRATT REMEMBERS THE CIRCUS

The small boy
with lanterns for eyes

whispered in the wings
of the dying circus.

He studied French
when not performing;

he hoped to do card tricks,
to travel in Europe,

his smile drifting
through the open door

of his soul.
The grifters

were awaiting the arrival
of the tent,

the hiring of the
roustabouts

who could
blend soft

Indian Summer days
into soft

buffalo nights and
the songs of Ephram Pratt.

EPHRAM PRATT TRAVELS AMONG UNKNOWN ISLES

Ephram Pratt is a silent,
inexpressive individual,

a dragonfly maybe,
or a praying mantis.

He has set his sights
on hunting water buffalo

on the African savanna,
visiting Iceland during Lent.

His voice is soft raisins
in a small box on the dresser,

kissed by an overdose
of whatever he wants.

Why does he want to sing
to the winter apples,

bought on a Jewish holiday
between visits to his therapist?

These are the questions
he poses when he prays,

when he visits the tenants
of his blind boarding house.

EPHRAM PRATT MEETS HIMSELF COMING AND GOING

Ephram Pratt sold
greeting cards

when he was young,
door to door,

a salve
for curing scabies,

acne, syphilis,
other minor irritations.

He discovered himself
inside the cover

of a Captain Marvel
comic: SHAZAM,

he'd shout, whenever
he made a sale.

Charles Atlas
drew him

into the pages
of his life, too,

whispering softly:
Ayn, Any Rand!

EPHRAM PRATT MEETS HIS DOPPELGÄNGER

He became a twin at 27,
meeting himself

in a shoe factory
in South St. Paul.

It was a surprise meeting;
he had just sworn allegiance

to Minnesota Public Radio,
when a voice came to him,

from an ancient crystal set
he carried in a small package

hidden inside
his left ear.

The voice whispered to him,
"I've known you

since before time began,
when we were one.

In the beginning was the Word,
and it was you and me."

The Word drifted off
into silence,

into a hard of hearing place,
where no one listened or cared,

but where twins communicate
in a language all their own.

EPHRAM PRATT SPEAKS IN THE LANGUAGE OF SEALS

He lived near the sea
and his days were filled

conversing softly with
deceased mermaids,

but from them
he learned

the language of seals,
the grunts, the whistles,

the body language,
the subtle eye movements.

The cottage on the cape
was filled with ancestors,

peopled with tiny clones
of whoever lived there.

Only in the shadows
did he allow himself to speak

the language he knew so well,
he loved so insanely.

Why should he not speak
with seals?

The language known by poets
since time began.

EPHRAM PRATT DISCOVERS THE *CHI* OF IMELDA MARCOS

He wanted new shoes.
Morning and evening

he would trudge
from shoe store

to shoe store,
quality being his

only criterion.
Oxfords, loafers,

hightops, sandals—
he didn't care.

He slept in his
track shoes

during April & May,
wishing his spikes

would come alive,
turn him into

a cheetah,
or a small rhino.

Imelda Marcos
became his hero.

He wanted to
sleep with her shoes,

to press them
into his navel,

letting her *chi*
enter his soul

through their shared
relationship of shoes.

EPHRAM PRATT REMEMBERS WHAT HE SHOULD FORGET

Ephram Pratt lives
a life of leisure.

He swims in the dark pools
of his own eyes,

sings love songs softly
to the Sirens of Syracuse.

His hands are soft
as daylight in the tropics,

like lemon covered
anecdotes in a weed garden.

Why do his songs,
his anecdotes,

his artichokes,
favor the lies

we learned as children?
The stories we were told

in the soft grasses
of childhood?

We know the answers,
but are afraid

to whisper them softly
into the ears of innocence,

into the caverns that
isolate us from winter.

EPHRAM PRATT READS NUMBERS IN THE SKY

Days were turning into fall
and Ephram Pratt

was counting the leaves
on the pepper plants

in his garden.
There were seventeen

on each plant,
a number meaningful

to members of
a secret society

headquartered
in Southern Sudan.

His gloved hands were red,
and he read

from a crimson scroll,
the red hair

of the Sirens of Syracuse
falling sensuously

over all the books,
from Nephi to Moroni,

scales falling from the eyes
of Salvador Dali

as he swam in the
sad rubicund ocean of salt.

EPHRAM PRATT REINCARNATES AS A SPIDER

There are times
when he works and plays

in the childhood
he has forgotten,

when the songs
he thinks he hears

are taken by
the scruff of his neck,

placed securely
in an antique box

and delivered piecemeal
to his imagination.

He may wonder
why the tapestry

he sees in the gallery
is seasoned with

a glowing tripod
of absolute nonsense,

but he sees
the luminous tapestry,

hears it, too,
and it makes him

want to lie down
in silence,

wondering if he will
reincarnate as an arachnid.

EPHRAM PRATT WILTS LIKE A BLACK TOOTH

It was late in the morning
when he arrived,

dark as half a zebra
leading into a maze,

a labyrinth actually,
like a centaur bleeding.

Late morning can be cold
as mangos in winter,

or warm, even hot,
like pus in a black tooth.

He dressed the way he did
because of the wandering Jew

he met circling the moat,
the one who had been

skulking around the outskirts
of the silk desert,

dreaming beef Bourguignon
laced with pain killers,

the ones he knew
nothing about,

but still standing, limping
within the twilight.

EPHRAM PRATT CONSIDERS PHONE CALLS HE NEVER MADE

The phone calls
he never made

were the ones
he never made;

they were the hardest,
the ones he meant to,

but didn't, couldn't,
or just postponed forever.

In them,
he heard sirens,

dial tones in impossible keys,
the sound of bubbles

sinking slowly
into the seas,

dancing on the stilts
of Buddha,

knowing nothing of
the pageantry of bliss.

It is what occurs
during the summer solstice,

that time when calls
from the other seasons

don't get answered,
but are silenced forever

by the invisible doors
of another childhood.

EPHRAM PRATT PONDERS THE BORDERLANDS

Worms and ferrets,
other small creatures,

bleeding into the Sartre-like
nothingness of time,

leaning over small
plastic soldiers

playing war games
on the kitchen floor.

Such abstractions surprise,
make one think of the past,

or of a portentous future
already held captive

in the cacophonous roar
of heavenly arrows and bullets.

I question such antediluvian
postponements—why?

Is it more important
for the nooses to hang loose

or the children of
the somber music

to ride rampant through
the borderlands,

slowly bringing the final days
into the present?

EPHRAM PRATT EXPERIENCES A BURNING JOY

Snow exiting holes in the sky,
leading legends into

the backhoe wilderness
of existence,

the elements eliciting
a fragrant joy

mixed with an elixir
of pungent rosemary

torn from the path
of incoming badgers,

raccoons, foxes,
and other wild things.

Is it because of
the pumping blood

that the vision we see
causes an erasure

of the sights and sounds
we first experienced

in those deaf moments
of grief and joy

we knew while
tendering soft prayers

into the sky
like burning grass?

EPHRAM PRATT EXTRAPOLATES ON THUNDER
EGGS

Word by word
and flower by flower

his words insinuate themselves
into a dying franchise,

his lips sealing the decades
of a brittle midnight.

He sings songs
he doesn't know at all,

but remembers
from a past life

as an amoeba, an ant,
or a thunder egg.

The final verse
is a cacophony

of bells, whistles
and human voices,

drifting into empty crevices,
abating the fringe

of a tasseled night train,
enveloped by an engineer

with tweed in his veins
from drinking too much wine.

EPHRAM PRATT BUILDS AN AMBIDEXTROUS LOGIC

Put your finger on it,
and pull the beautiful

and billowing fortress
along the lower river

in toward the shore;
let it sink slowly

in the shallows,
lying dormant

as an egg,
swallowed by incense

lingering in the shadow
of a wounded adder.

Don't let it fly unknown,
repeating slowly

what you know to be true,
what you know exists

in timelessness,
like the fingers on

your left hand, seeking
an ambidextrous logic,

invested in isolation
like a razor sulking.

EPHRAM PRATT PRATTLES ON ABOUT HOPE
& JOY

He softly places
his tiny box of hope

among the cinders,
but it doesn't burn,

only smolders,
like broken glass

in a cage of bliss,
causing small sparks

to fly into the air
on wings of silence,

on pennons
of crushed alabaster.

Friends attend
his mission

of attempting the future
with an avoidance

of missing liaisons,
with a silent bellow

clearly etched into
the sound of

his soul bleeding
from internal joy.

EPHRAM PRATT SINGS FROM THE WORD BOX

The word box,
brown and yellow

from leavings
found along the river,

bent with a small voice,
silently into

a wilderness
of crying trees.

It was the voice
of a wood fawn

that he heard
singing a full throated

no sound—
echoing like grass stains

violating the web
scribbled between

two voices
that don't exist,

or that exist
(maybe a little)

in the poet's mind,
like silk poems.

EPHRAM PRATT SINGS OF A SOLIPSISTIC FAILING

Solipsistic in nature,
the hands of the clock,

indeed, the fingers
on the hands

reaching into air,
into the silence

milling loosely
in a country of loss,

end in elegance,
like a poem

framed in silence.
Let it sing

in its strange
lilting voice

of sirens and sounds
belching from horns

and chimneys
reaching into the sky,

elegiac and beckoning
in a sound of ice,

in a system known
as failing,

a song known
as vacant, tuneless.

EPHRAM PRATT EXITS INTO SILENCE

Tucked into an opening
between silence

and nothing,
the signs on the burning

of a threadbare,
buoyant tunnel of air

sing with the voice
of a wilderness

plagued by ice,
an incendiary of bliss,

decaying soundlessly
above a cycle of cool jazz.

Let it mingle
with a juniper of joy,

tangling silently,
softly, with

brooches of turquoise
and jade,

blanketing the entrance
to a venerated wantonness

of doggerel,
elliptical and enduring.

EPHRAM PRATT IGNORES A CACOPHONY OF SILENCE

Intangible as a rock,
the work stands

enormous but silent,
like elk song

wading alive into
an unearthly silence,

relentlessly irreverent
and ignoring

the talisman found
along the road.

Why doesn't he ask
the questions

intoned in ancient
scriptures?

Weren't there victories
enough before

arrogant shackaleers
invaded the landing

and tore blue shells
of irradiated time

from balloon terrapins,
elegant in their

white cacophony,
renting the night air.

EPHRAM PRATT RECALLS THE SILENCE

Scurrying around like an eyeball
about to enter Scotland,

he wanders softly
into the darkness,

into shades of silence
not known to exist,

except by the dangerous ones,
the ones leaking oil & blood,

dying secretly
while no one watches.

Is it because of the
candle lighters,

the ones arching
into oblivion,

their shadows
white against an ageless

background of silence?
The ones with anger

melting into their voices
stand stark and stately,

unaware of the darkness
invading the silence.

EPHRAM PRATT REMEMBERS TIME IN THE GARDEN

Climbing the acorns of despair,
he reached into his pocket

and found sand,
sand the color of air,

clear, clean & drenched
in wisps of salt peter

and wine vinegar,
adding a strange luscious

quality to whatever
he mistook for reality.

Dangerous, it was
like wielding a cutlass

in the Garden of Eden,
softening the reach

of time as it flowed
into his slim silence,

guarding a mound of
blackberry bushes

growing in silence
behind the house on Mason,

like a glowing coal,
burnt into soft molasses.

EPHRAM PRATT EMITS OCTOBER CHANTINGS

Born like a stone
crossing time,

he emits willowy wisps
like the horns

of Broadway,
lined up like statues

issuing orders
to the saints of Melrose,

crossing their hearts
with dead fingers.

He erupts occasionally,
with a burst

of October chanting,
knowing his stockings

and other undiscovered
endeavors of science

won't last the winter,
but will disappear

like vagrant whispers
caught in the October winds

of a wilted Siberia,
aghast with fragrant

energy needles,
seeding the atmosphere

with tiny chevrons
of pure gold.

EPHRAM PRATT SURRENDERS TO SURREALISM

A   n ordinary
man   cultivating

is   not unlike
cut   ting grass

in   to a warm day
half   of which is living

by   the worms of nature,
a   mountain of sand

win   nowing in sadness,
dow   agers sleeping

a   nd rejecting knowledge
man   kind knows

is   not violable as is
cut   ting grass

in   an organdy glass
half   full of vapor, swung

by   closets closing doors
a   nd knots tied to

win   d sox absconding
dow   n empty stairs

EPHRAM PRATT COMPOSES A SESTINA

The sharp edges of his elbows etch miracles
Into the eyes of the neighbors filing papers
To have him recorded for posterity,
To have his innocence recorded in blue
Irises and roses, blossoming in silence,
Being sequestered by the poets singing.

You ask, petulantly, why are they still singing?
It's as if the weight of minor miracles
Dissolves into a nostalgic ellipse of silence
Fostered by an illusion of magic papers
Draped in shades and shards of diamond blue,
Strung and drugged into silence for posterity

Bleeding soft blood. The mention of posterity
Infuses ignorance into silence, singing
The absurd utterances of arrogant blue
Voices sliding softly into miracles,
Of books created from magic papers
Devoid of shackaleers preening in silence.

The voices in the back rows blend in silence,
Like poets held to face posterity,
The kind found in silent movies found in papers,
And never bathed in the virtue of singing
What artists and musicians label miracles,
Of actualizing shades of hyacinth blue

Baked into nothingness of a distant blue
Sky of minimalist composition. The silence
Of a thousand tiny errant miracles
Sings melancholy songs, a voice for posterity.
Voices tell us, however, it is the singing
Of the wicked notes etched on golden papers

Sliding silently over Tantalus, like papers
Dissolving into an acrimonious blue,
Bleeding like the faint eyes heard singing
The colors recorded in a blank silence,
Akin to what is found in posterity
Inching forward in a blaze of miracles.

He lingers singing, while mourning papers
Disguise false miracles in a blaze of blue,
Etched in ebullient silence, cast for posterity.

NOTES
An Introduction to Ephram

The Love Songs of Ephram Pratt came about as a result of my meeting Ephram Pratt some ten years ago.

I first met Ephram in a poem in 2008; I didn't know him previously & he is not related to a minor historical figure I've since encountered on the Internet. He is, in all likelihood, of the Tribe of Ephraim in the book of Numbers, and I also suppose he may be an alter-ego or doppelgänger of mine who talks and writes about things I may feel somewhat reluctant or uncomfortable in dealing with in my poems. Since meeting him, we have shared in writing some 800 of our "Songs of Ephram Pratt." Although I have been writing seriously since the late 1950s, the past several years, Ephram seems have monopolized the bulk of my writing time.

Ephram and I deal with subjects about which neither of us knows much of anything, as well as subjects on which one or both of us know a lot. We love to play with words and at times we love big long words that we just love to loll around on our tongues. We love to read them aloud, although I do most of the reading and Ephram just listens.

There are often times we write poems we don't know anything about, much less what they mean or understand them. Dali says, "The fact I myself do not understand what my paintings mean while I am painting them does not imply that they are meaningless." Ephram and I strongly agree with Dali, that just because we do not understand what our poems mean, it doesn't mean they are meaningless.

We believe in stream of consciousness, Kerouac's spontaneous prose and the dream world of Andre Breton's automatic writing.

Jack e Lorts
February 2019

ABOUT THE AUTHOR

Jack e Lorts, retired educator, lives in The Dalles, OR, via 20 years in Fossil, after stops in Kansas and California. He has published widely, if infrequently since the late 1950s, in such places as *Arizona Quarterly*, *Kansas Quarterly*, *English Journal*, more recently in *High Desert Journal*, *Fault Lines*, *Phantom Drift*, *Windfall*, and online such places as *Haggard and Halloo*, *Elohi Gadugi*, *Locust*, and *Eunoia Review*. Lorts is the author of three chapbooks, *The Daughter Poems & Others* and *The Meeting-Place of Words* (Pudding House 2008 & 2010) and *Dear Gilbert Sorrentino & Other Poems* (Finishing Line 2011). Active in Democratic and progressive politics, he has run for the Oregon House, served on the City Council and as Mayor of Fossil for many ensuing years.

He first published in the late 1950s alongside Ginsberg, Levertov, Padgett, Ted Berrigan, Russell Edson, Larry Eigner, and Cid Corman; he wonders what the hell happened in the ensuring years?

ACKNOWLEDGMENTS

Grateful acknowledgment is made to the editors of the following journals and presses for first publishing these poems or earlier versions of them:

Clackamas Literary Review. "Ephram Pratt Reads Numbers in the Sky." 2012.

Elementary, My Dear. "Ephram Pratt Remembers Time in the Garden." 2014.

Elohi Gadugi. "Ephram Pratt Ponders the Borderlands," 2013, "Ephram Pratt Wilts Like a Black Tooth," 2014, and "Ephram Pratt Emits Winter Chantings," 2015.

Fault Lines. "Ephram Pratt Meets His Doppelgänger," "Ephram Pratt Speaks in the Language of Seals," and "Ephram Pratt Discovers the *Chi* of Imelda Marcos." 2012.

Haggard and Halloo. "Ephram Pratt Extrapolates on Thunder Eggs," 2013, "Ephram Pratt Experiences a Burning Joy," 2013, "Ephram Pratt Builds an Ambidextrous Logic," 2013, "Ephram Pratt Sings of a Solipsistic Failing," 2015, "Ephram Pratt Exits into Silence," 2015, "Ephram Pratt Ignores a Cacophony of Silence," 2012, and "Ephram Pratt Composes a Sestina," 2014.

Literary Juice. "Ephram Pratt Sings of the Word Box." January, 2016.

Locust. "Ephram Pratt Considers the Phone Calls He Never Made." 2017.

Phantom Drift. "Ephram Pratt Surrenders to Surrealism." 2019.

The Taylor Trust. "Ephram Pratt Remembers the Circus," and "Ephram Pratt Travels among Unknown Isles." 2009.

COLOPHON

Titles for *The Love Song of Ephram Pratt* are set in Lucida Sans. Designed by Kris Holmes and Charles Bigelow in 1993, the font is designed to support the most commonly used characters defined in digital typography.

The body text itself is set in Garamond. It is a serif typeface, named for sixteenth-century Parisian engraver Claude Garamond.

Made in the USA
Middletown, DE
15 March 2019